EXPLORING THE STATES

Rhode Island

THE OCEAN STATE

by Amy Rechner

BELLWETHER MEDIA · MINNEAPOLIS, MN

Note to Librarians, Teachers, and Parents:

Blastoff! Readers are carefully developed by literacy experts and combine standards-based content with developmentally appropriate text.

Level 1 provides the most support through repetition of high-frequency words, light text, predictable sentence patterns, and strong visual support.

Level 2 offers early readers a bit more challenge through varied simple sentences, increased text load, and less repetition of high-frequency words.

Level 3 advances early-fluent readers toward fluency through increased text and concept load, less reliance on visuals, longer sentences, and more literary language.

Level 4 builds reading stamina by providing more text per page, increased use of punctuation, greater variation in sentence patterns, and increasingly challenging vocabulary.

Level 5 encourages children to move from "learning to read" to "reading to learn" by providing even more text, varied writing styles, and less familiar topics.

Whichever book is right for your reader, Blastoff! Readers are the perfect books to build confidence and encourage a love of reading that will last a lifetime!

This edition first published in 2014 by Bellwether Media, Inc.

No part of this publication may be reproduced in whole or in part without written permission of the publisher. For information regarding permission, write to Bellwether Media, Inc., Attention: Permissions Department, 5357 Penn Avenue South, Minneapolis, MN 55419.

Library of Congress Cataloging-in-Publication Data

Rechner, Amy.
  Rhode Island / by Amy Rechner.
    pages cm. – (Blastoff! readers. Exploring the states)
  Includes bibliographical references and index.
  Summary: "Developed by literacy experts for students in grades three through seven, this book introduces young readers to the geography and culture of Rhode Island"–Provided by publisher.
  ISBN 978-1-62617-039-1 (hardcover : alk. paper)
  1. Rhode Island–Juvenile literature. I. Title.
  F79.3.R44 2014
  974.5–dc23
                                                          2013008935

Printed in the United States of America, North Mankato, MN.

Table of Contents

Where Is Rhode Island?

Rhode Island is in the northeastern United States. It is part of **New England**. Massachusetts borders Rhode Island to the north and east. Connecticut is its western neighbor. More than 400 miles (644 kilometers) of coastline defines the southern edge of Rhode Island. The Atlantic Ocean washes onto its shores.

Rhode Island is the smallest state in the country. It is divided by Narragansett Bay. The capital and largest city is Providence. It is located at the top of the bay.

Atlantic Ocean

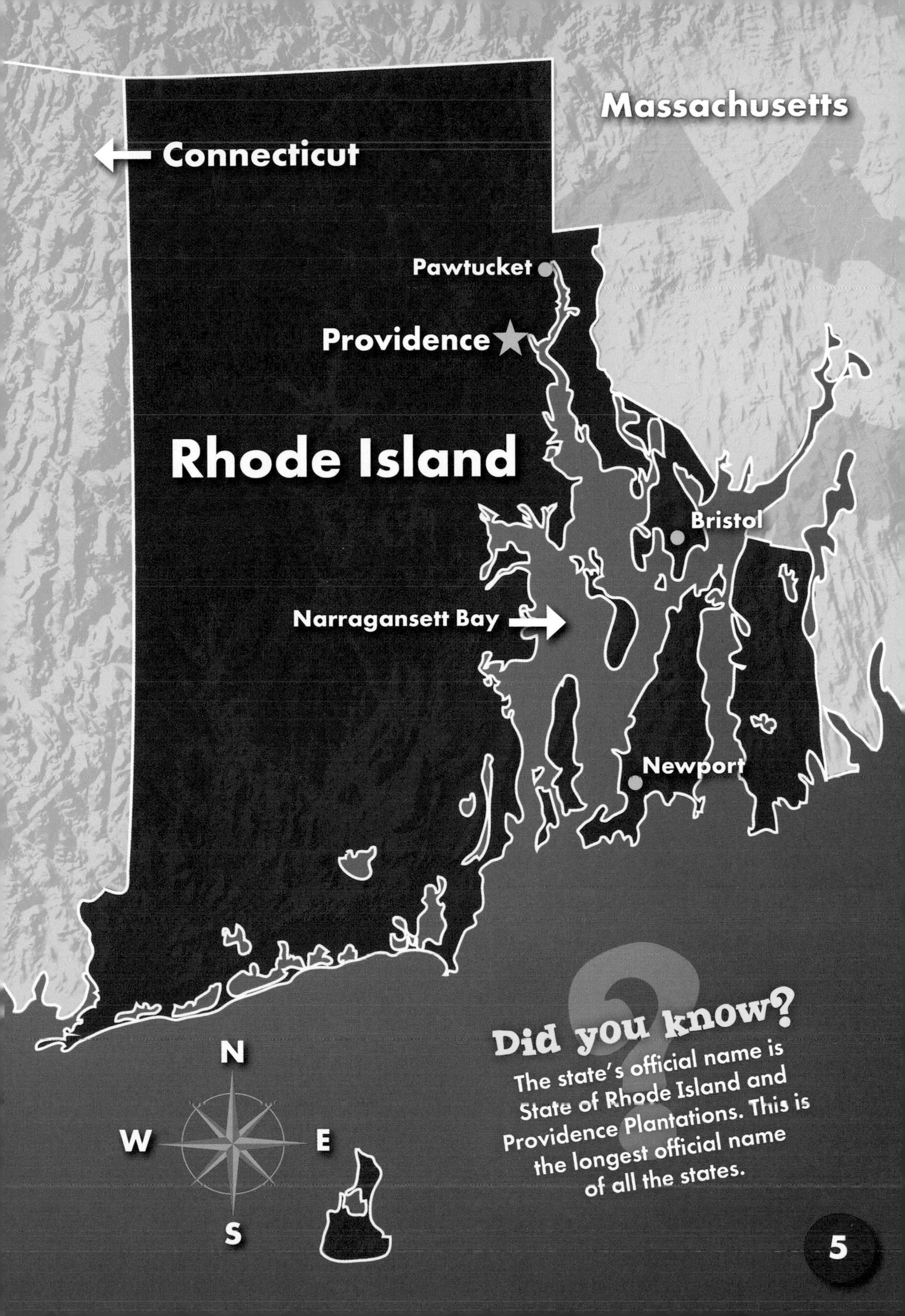

Massachusetts

Connecticut ←

Pawtucket ●

Providence ★

Rhode Island

Bristol ●

Narragansett Bay →

Newport ●

N
W   E
S

Did you know?

The state's official name is State of Rhode Island and Providence Plantations. This is the longest official name of all the states.

History

The Narragansett, Wampanoag, and other **Native** American tribes lived in Rhode Island before Europeans arrived. English **colonist** Roger Williams started Providence Plantations in 1636. In 1775, Rhode Island joined other **colonies** to fight for independence in the **Revolutionary War**. It became the thirteenth state in 1790.

Roger Williams and Narragansett Native Americans

Rhode Island Timeline!

1524: Italian explorer Giovanni da Verrazano sails into Narragansett Bay. He visits with Native Americans before leaving.

1636: Roger Williams starts a settlement called Providence Plantations.

1675-1676: Native Americans fight against colonists in King Philip's War. Several Rhode Island settlements are destroyed.

1772: Rhode Islanders set fire to the British ship HMS *Gaspee* in protest of King George III.

1790: Rhode Island becomes the thirteenth state.

1861-1865: Rhode Island fights for the North in the Civil War. Rhode Islander Ambrose Burnside is one of the leading Union generals.

1938: The Great New England Hurricane floods Providence and causes severe damage across Rhode Island. It is one of the worst storms ever to hit New England.

1978: The Narragansett tribe reclaims some of its land in Charlestown from the State of Rhode Island.

1996: A massive oil spill in Narragansett Bay kills thousands of lobsters and other wildlife.

HMS *Gaspee*

Ambrose Burnside

The Great New England Hurricane

The Land

Although it is small, Rhode Island has varied **terrain**. Rocky and sandy land borders the ocean and Narragansett Bay coasts. The state also includes several islands. Aquidneck, or Rhode Island, is the largest one. It lies in Narragansett Bay along with other smaller islands.

Farther inland, rivers wind through green, hilly land. The Blackstone and Pawtuxet Rivers connect historic towns and woodland trails. Forests filled with maple, oak, and elm trees blaze with colors in the fall. The cold winters thaw into pleasantly warm summers. Light ocean breezes sometimes turn into fierce winds or even **hurricanes**.

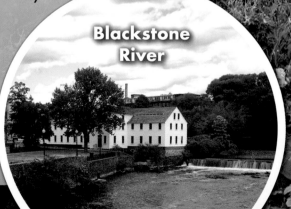

Blackstone River

Aquidneck Island

Rhode Island's Climate
average °F

spring
Low: 39°
High: 58°

summer
Low: 62°
High: 80°

fall
Low: 44°
High: 63°

winter
Low: 23°
High: 39°

Narragansett Bay

Narragansett Bay splits the state. Narrow strips of land lie on the east side. Most of the state is to the west. The bay has 256 miles (412 kilometers) of shoreline and many islands. No one lives on the smallest islands. Towns and villages fill Aquidneck and Conanicut, the largest islands. Many small harbors and **coves** break up the shoreline. Historic villages and lighthouses dot the coast.

tern

Beavertail
Lighthouse

Narragansett Bay is an
estuary. The mix of freshwater
and saltwater creates a unique environment
for plant and sea life. Prudence, Patience, and Hope
Islands have **nature reserves**. Plants and waterbirds
are protected on the islands.

Wildlife

blue shark

fun fact !

Blue, mako, and hammerhead sharks are sometimes spotted near Block Island and Narragansett Bay.

The thick forests of western Rhode Island are home to many kinds of wildlife. White-tailed deer, foxes, woodchucks, and raccoons seek shelter in the woodlands. Snowy owls hoot from the tree branches. Terns, herons, and other waterbirds search for food along the coast and on islands in the bay.

heron

quahogs

harbor
seal

The water is filled with life, too. Bass and trout swim in
lakes and rivers. Lobsters, crabs, and clams live in the
sea. A hard-shell clam called the quahog is especially
plentiful in Rhode Island. Finback and humpback whales
patrol the coastal waters. Harbor seals sun themselves
on warm rocks.

Landmarks

Despite its small size, Rhode Island has many interesting sights. The Slater Mill in Pawtucket is the country's first **cotton mill**. People can tour the original mill and a workman's house. At its machine shop, visitors see the mill's giant moving gears and water wheel. In Westerly, kids can ride the Flying Horse Merry-Go-Round. It was built in 1876!

Newport is home to a collection of mansions built in the 1700s and 1800s. **Tourists** go back in time as they walk through the grand rooms and gardens. Nearby Portsmouth boasts the Green Animals **Topiary** Garden. More than 80 trees and shrubs are shaped like elephants, bears, and other creatures.

Green Animals Topiary Garden

Newport mansion

Slater Mill

Providence

Rhode Island's capital city of Providence was founded in 1636. Since colonial times, **immigrants** came to the state to work. Much of Providence reflects these immigrant cultures. The Fox Point neighborhood has a large Portuguese population. Federal Hill has many Italian shops and restaurants.

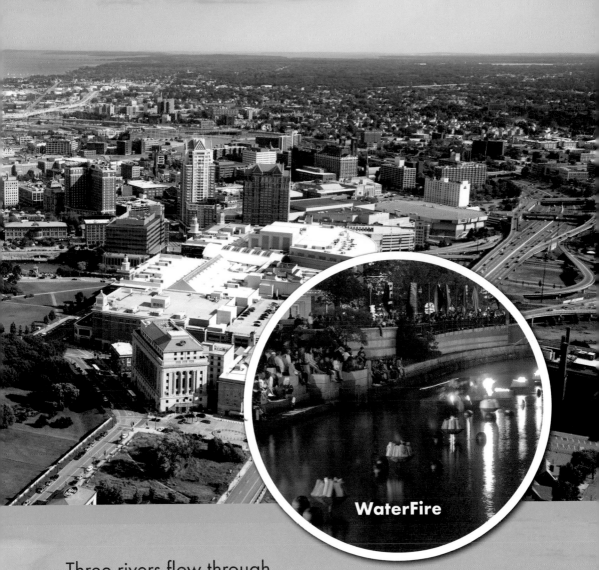

WaterFire

Three rivers flow through
downtown Providence. Throughout
the year, the city hosts an **urban** art event called
WaterFire. Bonfires cast glowing trails of light down
the middle of the rivers. People crowd the riverbanks to
experience WaterFire's music and fiery art exhibits.

Working

fun fact!

G.I. Joe and Mr. Potato Head are Rhode Islanders! They are both made by Hasbro, a toy company based in Pawtucket.

Rhode Island has a small number of farms. They produce dairy products, potatoes, and corn. Most Rhode Islanders have **service jobs**. Many work in **finance** or health care. They also serve the state's tourists in shops, hotels, and restaurants.

Manufacturing is also important to Rhode Island. Workers make **textiles**, silverware, and jewelry. Other factories produce metal products, electronics, and machinery. Off the coast, fishers fill their boats with shellfish. Lobster is the most valuable catch.

Where People Work in Rhode Island

government
12%

services
79%

farming and
natural resources
1%

manufacturing
8%

19

sailing

It is no surprise that Rhode Islanders love water sports. Sailing, swimming, and kayaking fill the summer days. Fishing is also popular. Sailboat races in Narragansett Bay draw crowds of viewers. College rowing teams compete on the Seekonk River.

Did you know?
The famous tennis competition now known as the U.S. Open started in Newport in 1881.

horseback riding

tennis

Rhode Island's many nature reserves attract hikers and bird-watchers. Horseback riding and bicycle trails cross the state. Athletes head to tennis courts when the weather is nice. In winter, people enjoy cross-country skiing, ice skating, and downhill skiing.

stuffed
clams

fun fact !

In Rhode Island, an ice cream
milkshake is called a cabinet.

Many unique foods come from Rhode Island.
Jonnycakes are cornmeal pancakes. The first settlers
made jonnycakes based on a Native American recipe.
The cakes are served with butter and syrup. Quahog
clams are cooked into **chowder**. They are also filled
with vegetables to make "stuffies." Doughboys are
chunks of deep-fried pizza dough sprinkled with sugar.

Rhode Island has some original drinks, too. Coffee milk
is a mixture of milk and sweet coffee syrup. Del's frozen
lemonade was first served from a stand in Cranston
in 1948.

Jonnycakes

Ingredients:

- 1 cup cornmeal
- 1 tablespoon sugar
- 1 teaspoon salt
- 1 cup boiling water
- 3 to 4 tablespoons milk

Directions:

1. Mix meal, sugar, and salt in large mixing bowl.

2. Add boiling water. Mix well.

3. Thin immediately with milk so mixture will drop easily from spoon. You may need to add more milk.

4. Drop by tablespoons onto hot, greased griddle. Add oil as needed to keep griddle greased.

5. Cook each side until browned. Serve with maple syrup and butter.

Festivals

Newport
Jazz Festival

Festivals are fun ways for Rhode Islanders to get together.
Warwick celebrates Gaspee Days to honor the early
victory over England. The event features a parade, a
model colonial army camp, and a burning ship. Bristol
hosts the nation's oldest Fourth of July celebration and
parade. This annual **tradition** began in 1785.

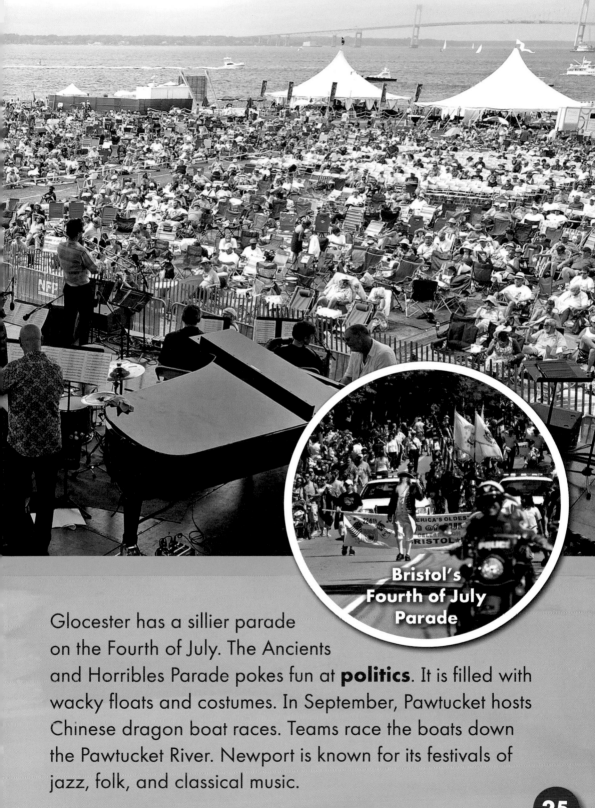

Bristol's
Fourth of July
Parade

Glocester has a sillier parade
on the Fourth of July. The Ancients
and Horribles Parade pokes fun at **politics**. It is filled with
wacky floats and costumes. In September, Pawtucket hosts
Chinese dragon boat races. Teams race the boats down
the Pawtucket River. Newport is known for its festivals of
jazz, folk, and classical music.

Clambakes

The clambake is a Rhode Island tradition. It began with the Wampanoag Native Americans. They developed the cooking method used for a clambake. The Wampanoag cooked clams, lobsters, oysters, and other shellfish over hot rocks.

The modern clambake usually takes place on the beach. Rocks are placed in a shallow pit and heated with burning wood. Then seaweed is put on top of the hot rocks. Racks of food are layered over the steaming seaweed. The food includes clams, corn, potatoes, and sometimes lobsters. The result is a delicious feast that everyone can enjoy. The clambake brings Rhode Islanders together to celebrate the state's rich past and bright future.

Fast Facts About Rhode Island

Rhode Island's Flag

Rhode Island's state flag is white with a golden anchor in the center. Thirteen stars surround the anchor. The stars represent the original colonies. Below the anchor is a blue ribbon with the state motto, "Hope."

State Bird
Rhode Island Red

State Nicknames:	The Ocean State The Plantation State Little Rhody
State Motto:	"Hope"
Year of Statehood:	1790
Capital City:	Providence
Other Major Cities:	Warwick, Cranston, Pawtucket
Population:	1,052,567 (2010)
Area:	1,221 square miles (3,162 square kilometers); Rhode Island is the smallest state.
Major Industries:	textiles, jewelry, tourism, fishing
Natural Resources:	fish, granite, limestone
State Government:	75 representatives; 38 senators
Federal Government:	2 representatives; 2 senators
Electoral Votes:	4

State Flower
blue violet

State Animal
striped bass

Glossary

chowder—a thickened soup made with seafood or vegetables

colonies—territories owned and settled by people from another country

colonist—a person who settles new land for their home country

cotton mill—a building with machinery that processes cotton into cloth

coves—sheltered areas where the shoreline dips inland

estuary—a place where a river meets the ocean

finance—the field of money management

hurricanes—spinning rainstorms that start over warm ocean waters

immigrants—people who leave one country to live in another country

manufacturing—a field of work in which people use machines to make products

native—originally from a specific place

nature reserves—lands that are set aside to protect animal homes and keep wildlife safe

New England—a group of six states that make up the northeastern corner of the United States

politics—the field of gaining power or influence in the government

Revolutionary War—the war between 1775 and 1783 in which the United States fought for independence from Great Britain

service jobs—jobs that perform tasks for people or businesses

terrain—the surface features of an area of land

textiles—fabrics or clothes that have been woven or knitted

topiary—the art of trimming trees and shrubs into shapes

tourists—people who travel to visit another place

tradition—a custom, idea, or belief handed down from one generation to the next

urban—relating to cities and city life

To Learn More

AT THE LIBRARY
Burgan, Michael. *Roger Williams: Founder of Rhode Island.* Minneapolis, Minn.: Compass Point Books, 2006.

Petreycik, Rick, and Lisa M. Herrington. *Rhode Island.* New York, N.Y.: Marshall Cavendish Benchmark, 2014.

Tieck, Sarah. *Rhode Island.* Minneapolis, Minn.: ABDO Pub. Co., 2013.

ON THE WEB
Learning more about Rhode Island is as easy as 1, 2, 3.

1. Go to www.factsurfer.com.

2. Enter "Rhode Island" into the search box.

3. Click the "Surf" button and you will see a list of related Web sites.

With factsurfer.com, finding more information is just a click away.

Index